About the Author

My name is Bella Cohen. I was born in Kishinev, Moldova in the former Soviet Union in 1957. My native tongue is Russian, and from a very early age I was influenced by amazing Russian poets, among them Anna Akhmatova and Marina Tzetaeva. I started writing poetry at twelve years old. When I turned sixteen years old, my family immigrated to Israel. There I majored in English Literature, and was introduced to many English and American poets, among them Emily Dickinson and Christina Rossetti. I have lived in the USA for the past forty years, teaching and writing. 'Soulful' is my second book of poetry.

Soulful

Bella Cohen

Soulful

Vanguard Press

VANGUARD PAPERBACK

© Copyright 2024
Bella Cohen

The right of Bella Cohen to be identified as author of
this work has been asserted by her in accordance with the
Copyright, Designs and Patents Act 1988.

All Rights Reserved

No reproduction, copy or transmission of this publication
may be made without written permission.
No paragraph of this publication may be reproduced,
copied or transmitted save with the written permission of the
publisher, or in accordance with the provisions
of the Copyright Act 1956 (as amended).

Any person who commits any unauthorised act in relation to
this publication may be liable to criminal
prosecution and civil claims for damages.

A CIP catalogue record for this title is
available from the British Library.

ISBN 978 1 80016 892 3

*Vanguard Press is an imprint of
Pegasus Elliot Mackenzie Publishers Ltd.*
www.pegasuspublishers.com

First Published in 2024

**Vanguard Press
Sheraton House Castle Park
Cambridge England**

Printed & Bound in Great Britain

I dedicate this book to love which is a source of inspiration for so many poets.

Acknowledgements

I would like to thank my wonderful aunt, Polina Rozentul for exposing me to poetry from early childhood. I would also like to thank my cousin, Luba Gurarie, who enthusiastically encouraged me to submit my poems for publication.

Contents

Can't Write Without Inspiration	15
With a Whiff of a Magic Wand	16
Is Love Just an Illusion?	17
Away From You	18
My Heart is Still	19
The Beam of Our Affection	21
I am Attached to You	22
And When I See You	23
I Yearn for a Quiet Happiness	24
What Doesn't Kill You	25
You're Far Away	26
Roads that Weren't Taken	27
I Want to Hold You	28
My Secret	29
Your Presence is Absence	30
Illicit Affairs	31
Waiting for Your Call	33
Long-Distance Relationships	34
Officially Old	35
The Final Frame	37
To See Inside Your Soul	38
My Four Loves	39
Aging with Grace	40
The Irony of Life	41
Obsessive Thoughts	42
Don't Believe Your Thoughts	43

She Shed Her Tears	44
They Suddenly Grew Old	45
Life is a Play	46
Love the Bad Away	47
Fragile, like a Crystal Vase	48
He Left	49
Men Are Amazing Creatures	50
When Things End	51
Time Will Pass	52
We are a Mystery	53
I Live all Alone	55
My Heart is Empty	56
You're Tired	57
Lack of Synergy	58
I Live in Magic	59
She Loved and Loved	60
An Iceberg	61
In the Window	62
My Soul Needs a Compass	63
Expiry Date	64
Emotions	65
Dancing Together	67
Let the Past Go	68
An Old Man in the Desert	69
Another Day	70
A Dark and Gloomy Day	71
Time Glides Slowly	72
A Wilted Brown Leaf	73
Like the Swallow and Thumbelina	74

You Are My Sin	76
In the Light of the Day	77
Younger than Me	78
At My Mature Age	80
Living Apart	82
At Last	84
My 65th	85
If I Only Had Today	86
And Suddenly I'm Calm	87
When I Leave this World	88

1
Can't Write Without Inspiration

Can't write
Without inspiration
From doubts,
Silent contemplations,
From life or love in disarray,
From disappointments
On my way.
I guess
Each poet needs to feel
Rage, misery or loss
Until
They can express
Their emotions
Through their poetry,
No caution,
Just words
Like tears on a page,
Releasing feelings
From its cage.

2
With a Whiff of a Magic Wand

With a whiff
Of a magic wand,
With a word
From a magic spell,
With a prayer
From sacred books,
With a wish
At the wishing well,
I can make you
Think about me;
I can make you
Love me so much;
I can make you
Dream of me nightly;
I can make you
Yearn for my touch.
But if my spell dissipates,
And my wishes
Lose their powers,
Will you still
Love me and care?
Will you still
Bring me beautiful flowers?

3
Is Love Just an Illusion?

Is love just an illusion,
A creation of one's soul
That needs to feel belonging
Because it hates to be alone?
Is love a mad obsession,
Or paradise on earth?
It makes a person
Wish for death
Or dance around in mirth.
Can love be an elixir,
Sweet potion
Of one's dreams,
Or poison
That destroys your heart?
It can be both, it seems.
It is a blessing
And a curse,
A feather
And a knife.
But only love
Can light your soul
Like nothing else in life.

4
Away From You

Away from you,
My lover — friend,
Across the ocean,
Hazel blue,
I thought of you,
My hopeless love
And wondered
If you miss me too.
I fear
One day you'll dissipate
Like in the morning
Quivering haze,
And I will never
Hear your voice
Or see your smiling face.

5
My Heart is Still

My heart is still,
No sudden palpitations,
No joy or happiness
That make you want to fly,
No disappointments,
No elations
And no more painful
Lows and highs.
It's calm and quiet.
Rhythm is steady.
The pulse is like
A well-wound clock.
It doesn't skip a beat
Or tremble.
It's numb, serene —
A silent rock.
The absence of love
Might be healthy
For a heart
That's worked so long.
But how I wish
To shed a tear

While listening
To a sad love song.
Just one last time
To fall in love,
Just one last time
Might be enough.

6
The Beam of Our Affection

The beam of our affection
Lingered in between us
For many, many years,
As brightly as could be.
But now its light's depleted
By obstacles and hardships
And thousands of miles
Dividing you and me.
No miracles to hope for.
Designed by higher power,
Our life maps don't include
Each other, not at all.
We only have our memories,
To think of and remember,
While we are separated
By the fateful wall.

7
I am Attached to You

I am attached to you
Like leaves attach
To their branches
In early spring.
It's a wonderful thing
To know that the wind,
A treacherous fiend,
Cannot carry me away.
I want to stay
By your side.
Forever…

8
And When I See You

And when I see you
I'll exhale
The year
Of longing, of regret,
Of all the moments
Left untouched,
Of all the tests
We both have failed.
I will exhale it
With a kiss,
A deep kiss,
One
You won't forget,
One
That will quickly dissipate
Our every doubt and regret.

9
I Yearn for a Quiet Happiness

I yearn
For a quiet happiness,
Lazy mornings
With you by my side,
The enticing smell
Of strong coffee,
Gentle breeze blowing in
Wrapped in light,
Orange blossoms,
Intoxicating,
Peeking in
Through white curtains of lace,
And you kissing me
Gently, softly
As my hand's
Caressing your face.

10
What Doesn't Kill You

It seems
We all have challenges,
Life's never carefree.
They say:
"What doesn't kill you
Will make you strong,
You'll see."
By now I should be Samson
With a flowing mane of hair.
Yet I feel older, weaker,
Which seems to me unfair.
Discords and sleepless nights
Have taken their toll.
I hope
What doesn't kill me,
Won't kill me after all.

11
You're Far Away

You're far away.
No need to pray.
No sense in shedding tears.
As years pass
I'll suffer less
From haunting dreams
And fears,
Until you sink
Like a golden ring
Into my memory's well
And disappear,
Lost and gone,
No stories left to tell.

12
Roads that Weren't Taken

Roads that weren't taken,
Goals that weren't met,
Love that was forsaken —
You can't help but fret.
You have good intentions,
To your plans adhere,
Until surprising
Fate or chance
Decide to interfere.
It's hard to live your life
Without expectations.
So, do your best,
Accept the rest
To avoid frustrations.

13
I Want to Hold You

I want to hold you
In my arms
And feel your breath
On mine.
I want to drown
In your charms
And cross
Forbidden lines,
And to forget
What's wrong or right
And do just what I feel.
But then I wake up
And you're gone,
Yet love
Is here…still

14
My Secret

You will be my secret.
I'll hide you
Deep inside
Like squirrels
Bury acorn seeds
In soil
Out of sight.

15
Your Presence is Absence

Your presence is an absence…
At least it feels like that.
We sit together in silence,
The mood is tense and sad.
Somewhere else already,
We try to comprehend
How we came to be here,
Once lovers, caring friends,
Today, two total strangers,
Our souls detached for good.
Love doesn't last forever.
How much I wish it would!

16
Illicit Affairs

Illicit affairs
Don't turn into love.
Shaky like quick sand,
They are seldom enough.
Most of the time
You're left disappointed
By a lover who feels
That he is anointed
To manage your time
And your emotions
With phone calls,
Sweet words
His magic potion.
He wants to forget
Bad things in his life,
Like too much stress
Or a nagging wife.
If you expect more
From this flimsy connection,
He'll keep you in place
By alienation,
By being indifferent and cold,
Until you act

As you've been told.
Why would anyone
Walk in quicksand?
Yet many do…
Towards the pitiful end.

17
Waiting for Your Call

I am waiting for your call…
It may never come.
The relationship
Is futile,
Bad for everyone.
Still, we push
This cart uphill,
Only God knows why,
Well aware
That one day
It will go awry,
Crushing both of us
Like ants
With its heavy weight …
But I still stare
At the phone,
Wondering
Why you're late.

18
Long-Distance Relationships

Long-distance relationships
Seldom work.
Why are we wasting our time?!
Find a woman you trust.
Love's not always a must.
And you'll be,
No doubt,
Just fine.

She'll take care of you,
She'll be there for you,
Not like me
Who is too far away.
You'll forget me,
I'm sure.
Time is often a cure.
"Out of sight, out of mind"
Wise men say.

19
Officially Old

There is no going back,
I'm officially old.
No time machine
Reversing age,
I'm told.
And even if offered
I won't agree
To go back in time,
Even for free.
Life is a journey
With its ups and downs,
Hills and ravines,
Deep holes in the ground.
We rise and we fall,
And rise once more.
Every day — a new chance
We were hoping for.
If death never came
Our life will resemble
A broken record,
No surprise, no gamble,
No excitement, anticipation,

No conclusion or contemplation,
Just more of the same:
Day, night, day, night
With nothing interesting
In sight.

20
The Final Frame

It's done, it's over,
Finished with,
Drowned
In the past.
You disappeared
From my screen.
The final frame, at last.

21
To See Inside Your Soul

My skill
To see inside your soul
Is an awful affliction.
I'd rather believe
You adore me,
Like in romantic fiction.
But it's clear to me
That your feelings,
Like dew in the sun,
Dried up.
Love is a flower
That needs to be watered,
But you…stopped.
Indifference and boredom
Grew weeds
Inside your soul.
And just like that —
Your love is gone
And I'm left all alone.

22
My Four Loves

Four chambers of my heart
Are filled up to the rim
With four loves in my life,
Some vivid still, some dim.
I'm grateful, no complaints.
No room for someone new.
To love and to be loved
God grants to just a few.

23
Aging with Grace

You can't run away
From 'old age',
No matter
How hard you try;
No matter
How many Botox shots
You get around your eyes;
No matter
How many surgeries
You put your body through;
You'll be considered elderly
No matter what you do.
Men will still ignore you,
Mirrors will still disappoint.
You will become way poorer,
Yet, old age you won't avoid.
Aging is a natural process.
Don't torture your body and face.
Growing old is not shameful,
If it's done with grace.

24
The Irony of Life

Why are those
We love the most
Often far away,
Yet those who tend
To mar our life
Close to us remain?
The irony of life,
The trickery of fate,
The mystery of chance.
Who knows
What's on your plate?
It seems
One has to suffer
To enter Heaven's gate.

25
Obsessive Thoughts

Obsessive thoughts
And sleepless nights,
An ocean full of tears,
Laments of sadness
And despair
Will land you on deaf ears
Of those who are unwilling
To compromise with you,
And look for just solutions,
Often overdue.
When things are out of your control,
And you hit a dead end,
Release, move on, and heal yourself.
Some things you cannot mend.

26
Don't Believe Your Thoughts

In sadness, anger or despair,
When you feel lonely,
Scorned or lost,
When those you love
Seem to ignore you
Your psyche always suffers most.
You start believing silly stories
Your brain's creating in defense:
My lover cheats,
My friends don't care,
Or other tales
That make no sense.
Perhaps your lover's been too busy,
Your friend has fallen gravely ill.
Yet, you continue getting angry
Believing everything you feel.
It's hard to tell sometimes
What's real
Or simply made up
In your head.
'Do not believe
Each thought you're thinking.'
Once someone wisely said.

27
She Shed Her Tears

She shed her tears
Into the sea
And sighed her sadness
To the winds.
Her dreams
She drowned in red wine.
Can she atone
For all her sins?
She keeps her secrets
From the world.
No one should know
What's in her soul.
She'll love in silence
Till she dies…
Probably alone.

28
They Suddenly Grew Old

They suddenly grew old,
Like other things in nature.
Nothing stays the same
On our Earth... Alas.
Once energetic, sprightly,
Eager to move mountains,
They're sitting on a couch,
No energy, no sass.
Their shoulders close together,
Their arms entwined like branches,
They are looking at each other
With tenderness and love.
The past is far behind them,
They're left with tender memories
Of times worth going back to.
For them, it is enough.

29
Life is a Play

At times I feel
That life is a play,
We are actors
Performing on stage.
We follow the script
Sometimes, improvise,
Scene after scene,
Page after page.
Some of the people
Are wonderful actors,
Doing what
They're required to do.
Some are less talented,
Making mistakes,
And paying the price
For not acting on cue.
We wake up each morning
And start a new chapter
With a hot cup of coffee,
And a hope that the day
Will go on as scripted,
Without bad surprises,
Or sudden misfortunes
Along our way.

30
Love the Bad Away

You cannot love
The bad away,
Like rain absolves the air.
You'll waste your efforts
And your heart
On those
Beyond repair.
You will imagine
In your brain
That things
Are getting better.
He might act nicer
For a while,
But then
Your hopes
Will shatter.
He will be back
To his old ways,
Unless you are aware
That you can either
Change yourself,
Or once more
Face despair.

31
Fragile, like a Crystal Vase

Fragile like a crystal vase,
Transparent like a drop of dew,
Passionate like a hurricane,
Is my love for you.
Gentle like a summer breeze,
Potent like a magic brew,
Complex like a cornfield maze,
Is my love for you.
But if you treat me
With indifference,
My love will lose
All its magnificence.

32
He Left

He left…
And suddenly each sound
Seems louder at night.
There's nobody to talk to,
To laugh with or to fight.
She eats her meals in silence,
Sits on her coach alone,
Staring into distance,
Past the silent phone.
Nobody to watch with,
Movies and the news,
No one to discuss with,
Differences in views.
Silence and more silence,
Just sirens in the distance.
He's gone — the only witness
To her whole existence.

33
Men Are Amazing Creatures

Men are amazing creatures.
They love themselves as they are.
They look in the mirror with pride:
"I look like a movie star."
While women gaze with displeasure
At their reflection each day.
"Look at these horrible wrinkles,
I wish I could wipe them away.
My nose is pretty crooked,
Much too big for my face.
These huge belly and thighs —
Unquestionable disgrace.'
To strife for perfection is pointless,
Because it doesn't exist.
Love yourself as you are,
And dispose of the
'What's wrong with me' list.

34
When Things End

There are times
When things end,
Unexpectedly, simply,
Like when someone dies
And vanishes quickly.
Like, in marriages,
When someone is done
They get a divorce,
And they're suddenly gone.
Pain, heartache, trauma
Linger behind.
Life can be hard
And often unkind.
But the end of something,
Is often a start,
Of hope, better future,
And a new love
In your heart.

35
Time Will Pass

Time will pass by
If you love me.
Clocks will chime
If you don't care.
Earth will spin
If you desert me,
Or if you are there.
We are little specks of dust
In this world, so grand,
And no matter what we feel,
Things will move as planned.

36
We are a Mystery

We are a mystery
To others
And to ourselves,
A book, unread
In a shiny cover,
Sitting on a shelf.
No one is privy
To our essence.
Even we can't tell
What we're capable of doing
If things
Don't go too well.
If we are crossed
Or angered,
Under great duress,
Acts we choose
To do sometimes
Are anybody's guess.
We hope
That our common sense
Along with a moral code,
Will lead us

In the right direction
Along life's
Treacherous road.

37
I Live all Alone

I live all alone
In my small lovely place,
Just me and my thoughts,
Soft light on my face.
It streams through the curtains
During the day.
It fills me with peace,
Takes my worries away.
My home is a place
Of refuge, of rest,
Where I can relax,
Free of all the stress.
Just me with myself,
Books on a shelf,
Coffee and wine,
Dark chocolate so fine,
A comfy coach to rest,
And peace that lasts.

38
My Heart is Empty

My heart is empty
Like a crystal glass,
That waits for love
To fill its yearning space
With dark red wine
That can intoxicate
Whoever's brave enough
This glass to raise.

39
You're Tired

You are tired,
Exhausted by life,
Its demands and trials,
No end.
You cannot sustain
One more plight,
One more problem
Out of hand.
You want peace,
Nothing weighing you down.
Fishing somewhere,
Deep in the sea.
Or napping alone
In a hammock,
Hanging low
From a coconut tree.
Peace,
Whisper of waves,
Tranquility
And infinity… infinity…

40
Lack of Synergy

All we ever felt
And knew
Would always be,
All of a sudden
Vanished
From lack of synergy,
From rarity of contact,
Mind to mind connection.
We're left to entertain
Resentment
And frustration.
It's hard
To end it all.
It's hard
To get it right.
So we just trot in place,
Solution's out of sight.

41
I Live in Magic

I live in magic
And feed on dreams.
I taste sour juices
Flowing through trees.
I bathe
In the blue sky,
Clear like dew,
Feeling the sun's warmth
And thinking of you.
You are also my dream.
And like a dream
You are gone
With the song of a swan.
I am left all alone,
Dropping tears in the wind,
Lonely like me.
That is sighing in sadness,
Unwillingly free.

42
She Loved and Loved

She loved and loved
And loved him
With all her heart and soul.
For days and months and years
He strung her along.
And then,
One sunny morning,
As she lay wide awake,
She realized her ardent love
Had become an arid lake.
No storms,
No rains,
No lightning.
A cloudless sky above.
'How nice!'
She sighed in solace,
Glad
To fall out of love.

43
An Iceberg

Lying at night
All alone,
An iceberg
Afloat on the sea,
Drifting slowly
To nowhere
For days,
Wishing
You were here with me,
Your warmth
Engulfing my soul,
Your touch
Breathing life into me,
But just like a ship
On the waves,
You are gone
In the mist of the sea.

44
In the Window

In the window
She stands
Looking out
At the trees
Shedding leaves in the rain,
To the sound
Of a passionate wind,
Wailing and sighing in pain.
Like an Ancient Roman sculpture,
Silently staring ahead,
Immersed
In mysterious thoughts,
She appears
Pensive and sad.
Broken hopes, lost love,
Disappointments —
Who knows
What's troubling her soul,
As she's standing there
In silence,
Mysterious
As the fall.

45
My Soul Needs a Compass

My soul needs a compass
That will show it direction.
I feel lost these days,
Lacking connection
To a place,
To people I am around.
My mind is fluttering,
No feet on the ground.
To write, to teach, to volunteer?
Crossroads of sorts,
Nothing is clear.
But perhaps, just for once
I should try living free,
No compass or captain,
A boat on the sea.
And me being me.

46
Expiry Date

River beds dry out,
Rain and storms do end,
Ripened fruits fall down,
And ruins drown in sand.
Flowers wilt in autumn.
Death is seldom late.
Every living thing
Has an expiry date.
Things will end one day,
To be replaced in time
By many new creations,
Man-made and divine.
Butterflies emerge
From new cocoons each day,
And pretty flowers blossom
Each spring along the way.

47
Emotions

Emotions
Are the crushing waves,
Wind
On a summer day,
Tornadoes
Twisting through the field,
Destruction in their way.
Emotions
Are the burst of rays,
Eruptions of great force,
A sand storm
Twirling through the desert
On its collision course.
But what I feel for you
Is light,
Just like a cloud floating by.
And what I feel for you
Is deep,
Just like the air in the sky.
And what I feel for you
Is bright,
Just like the golden sun above.

And what I feel for you
Is strong,
A strong emotion
I call 'Love.'

48
Dancing Together

Dancing together
Like one,
Swaying to music
Slowly.
An elderly couple's immersed in each other…
Wholly.
Dancing,
She plays with his hair,
Grayish and thin
Like a thread.
He lovingly looks in her eyes,
Teary a bit,
And content.
To them,
Each day is important.
Death might be
Down the street.
In tender embrace
They dance,
In sync,
Their souls
And their feet.

49
Let the Past Go

She tried to leave
Her past behind…
Unsuccessfully.
It interfered with her life,
Refused to set her free.
So, she continued going back
And forth and back again,
Always trying to move on,
Yet, seemingly, in vain.
Perhaps, she felt a bit too old
To overcome her doubts,
Finally succumbing,
As sad as it may sound.

50
An Old Man in the Desert

An old man
In the desert,
Resting on a stone.
Everyone he knew
Is dead.
He is left all alone.
No need
To wake up early,
There's nowhere to go.
Every single hour
Is tedious and slow.
Right time to contemplate
His life that's almost done,
Remember times of joy,
Misery and fun,
Days one wants to cherish,
Some others to forget.
With life is but behind him,
No reason for regret.
He gazes at the clouds,
Floating high above.
He learnt one thing
In his long life:
All living things need love.

51
Another Day

Another day,
Another light,
Another chance,
Another fight,
Another smile,
A bit of fear,
A little sadness,
A salty tear.
A little happiness
Inside,
Another wrong,
Another right,
Another day,
A glimpse of hope
To move ahead,
Pulled by the rope
Of time…
Another day,
Another night,
Some things go wrong,
Some things go right.

52
A Dark and Gloomy Day

A dark and a gloomy day,
Drizzle outside,
Grey clouds in the sky,
Swallowing the light.
I feel moody and impatient,
Sick of messages of hope.
War's somewhere,
Climate warming,
Who'll extend us all a rope?
I refuse to think about it.
I don't wish to contemplate
Which disaster can be halted,
Or for which it's way too late.
But today I'll sit around,
Watch reality TV,
And forget all earthly issues.
Movies, popcorn,
And just me.

53
Time Glides Slowly

Time glides slowly
Like a snail
If you have to sit in jail,
Or you do a boring a job,
Or clean a house
For a slob.
If you go
On an awful date,
Wait for someone
Who is late;
Do a chore
Not to your taste,
Time will drag and drag…
No haste.

But when you are happy,
Having fun,
Time will definitely run.
If you beg it to slow down,
It won't even turn around.
This is simply how it is:
Lasting pain
And jiffy bliss.

54
A Wilted Brown Leaf

She's like
A wilted brown leaf,
Suspended
On a bare tree,
Weary
Of every gust of wind,
Afraid
Of being free,
Of breaking loose,
Of flying wild
To foreign lands,
Towards something strange.
She'd rather
Hang there
By herself,
On her familiar branch.

55
Like the Swallow and Thumbelina

Like the Swallow
And Thumbelina,
That escaped
From the evil mole,
She is willing
To find her freedom
And reclaim her soul.
She is ready
To gather strength,
To allow her
To break away
From his coldness,
And his anger,
From his threats
And looks that slay.
She succeeded
To cross the threshold
Of the door
Ajar too long,
Overcoming every fear
That had kept her
From being strong.

She will not say goodbye,
No need to.
Her departure
Is overdue.
With her misery
At her feet,
She walks through the door…
Adieu!

56
You Are My Sin

You are my sin
And my salvation.
You are my bliss
And condemnation.
You are my truth,
You are my lie.
You make me laugh,
You make me cry.
You drive me mad,
You bring me peace.
You can torment,
You can appease.
I say goodbye,
I say hello.
You're on my mind,
I can't let go.
The seesaw
Will go up and down
Until all screws
Fall on the ground.

57
In the Light of the Day

Come to me
In the light of the day,
In the sunray
That crushes the sea.
Touch me
With the softness of waves,
In the lashes of rain
Come to me.

58
Younger than Me

Before my face
Is furrowed with wrinkles
And droopy eyelids
Hang over my eyes,
Before my hair
Gets grey and brittle,
I want to see you
One more time.
Before my lips
Get thin and discolored,
And my teeth
Turn yellow with age,
I want to kiss you
Passionately,
Like lovers kiss on stage.
Before my bones
Give in to arthritis.
And my legs
Hurt when I move,
I want to have
A last dance with you.
Together in the groove.

We can break
All the clocks around,
Throw our watches
Into the sea,
But time will continue running
And you'll always
Be younger than me.

59
At My Mature Age

I hoped,
At my mature age,
I would know quite well
What deeds
Would lead me into heaven,
What sins
Straight into hell.
However,
I am still confused about
What I want and why;
Whom to leave
And whom to love,
I cannot decide.
Still hopelessly romantic,
I know without a doubt
I need to make decisions
With both feet
On the ground.
I really hope
I can achieve
Peace
Within my soul.

And live in harmony
With myself
Until the final call.

60
Living Apart

We have never
Lived together,
But I wonder
If it's true,
That if we had
Moved in together,
I would start
Ignoring you.
We'd quit
Kissing one other,
Passionately like today.
You would not say
That you miss me
If I had to go away.
I would not
Caress you gently
When I lie with you
In bed.
You'd forget to say:
"I love you."
Which would make me
Way too sad.

If I share
My dreams and stories,
I would bore you
From the start.
So, because I love you, dear,
We should always
Live apart.

61
At Last

At last
We love each other
The way we always should have,
With kindness and with warmth
That melt my heart away.
With clear understanding
That, though we might be different,
We have to leave our problems
And attitudes at bay.
We try to listen better
And pause before reacting.
Impulsive answers lead
To anger and discord.
We cherish our union
At this stage
More than ever.
To lose each other now,
We simply can't afford.

62
My 65th

I greeted my 65
Without regret or tears.
So much
Has changed in my life
In the last few years.
I am older and wiser now,
I strive to enjoy each day.
I don't think about tomorrow
Though it's only one day away.
I stay in the present moment,
I try not to sweat the small stuff
I savor each drop of coffee,
Each instant with people I love.
I take time to smell the flowers,
Watch clouds across the sky.
At my age I am well aware
How fast life can pass you by.

63
If I Only Had Today

If I only had today,
It better be
The best of days,
The sunny one,
With rainbow clouds,
With a tender wind
That blows my way.
I'd like to see
The birds above
And butterflies
Around me;
Soft waves
Caressing grainy sand.
Me,
Dozing underneath a tree.
I hope to be surrounded
By people that I love.
To spend
A joyous day with them
Will surely be enough
To make that day
A perfect day…
But I don't always
Get my way.

64
And Suddenly I'm Calm

And suddenly I'm calm,
My hand is in his palm,
Its warmth is reassuring
Like a Bible psalm.
His mighty, manly hand,
Crossed with bulging veins,
Heals everything that bothers me,
All my aches and pains.
I tightly squeeze his hand,
Not wanting to let go…
I close my eyes,
I feel at peace.
Because I love him so.

65
When I Leave this World

When I leave this world
I will hover above,
Like a beautiful butterfly
To protect those I love.
I will gaze at the world,
Struggling below,
And I'll deeply sigh,
Soaked in heavenly glow.
I'll be safe from anger,
Earthly highs and lows.
I'll feel only compassion
Toward the ones below.
When I'm done protecting
Those dear to me,
I hope the Creator
Sets me finally free.